Copyright © Leila Chalk 2017
Photographs Copyright © Andrew Chalk 2017
Author Leila Chalk
Art Direction Andrew Chalk
Recipes Hajro Dizdar, Edina Dizdar nee Paravlić, Edina Bošnjak nee Dizdar,
and Leila Chalk nee Bošnjak

First Edition

Web: www.leilachalk.com
Instagram: @leila.chalk
Facebook: www.facebook.com/bosniancooking

Dizdar, throughout the Ottoman Empire, was the fortress commander. The Dizdar was expected to feed his people.

Written by The Chef's niece, this book is about a man who got lost in a war.

It is about the food that he cooked, and the journey that he did not get to take. Since the early 1990s the cuisine of Bosnia was left unexplored as people fought starvation. Its chefs, like all its artists, found other ways to feed their families. After the dust settled, it felt like the world had left us behind. Thousands of projects now exist, much like this one, to advance artistic expression. The purpose of this project is to give back one man his voice; and his chef's knives.

Introduction by the Chef's Niece

My earliest memories of my uncle are about food. The smell of freshly baked bread, the textures of crisp vegetables, foraging in old growth forests; learning.

In the late 1980s my uncle ran a restaurant on the northern border of Bosnia, called Boem. There, he often fed me the wonders of the world and told me they were chicken. I was a terror of a child, a picky eater, having grown up surrounded by chefs and fine cooks.

The crucible of my childhood was the war that betrayed our region in the early 1990s. It is in this darkness that my uncle became the Lost Chef, and that my intricate relationships with food were forged.

Untangling them now is complicated. Distinguishing modern Bosnian cuisine is equally a private and publicly necessary affair. Modern life has changed in such ways that each kitchen and pantry must now adapt to new lifestyles and new palettes.

In 2007 I visited during summer and insisted on trying that afternoon's homemade plum jam with the barbecued chicken The Chef was making. The family was instantly in uproar. Sweet and savoury food never mixed in Bosnian homes. Our forays in this flavour profile have stood at a standstill for it had been many decades since Nana had made her "honeyed meats" for a local culinary exhibition. (No honey was used; it is a stew made with rich local prunes – see page 106).

Modern Bosnian cuisine must bridge this gap – and endless others. There is much to be said for a good plum sauce, for sultanas in a pilav, and for sour cream on every cake.

Contents

Ajvar	6
Puter sa Biberom	8
Čilbur	10
Nanini Krompirčići	12
Punjene Paprike	14
Pečene Paprike	16
Pura	18
Somun	20
Kiflice sa Lukom	22
Lepine	24
Pogača	26
Uštipak	28
Fildžanuša	30
Kašikača	32
Kljukuša	34
Mutuša	36
Jufka	38
Burek	40
Mantije	42
Zeljanica	44
Krompiruša	46
Masirača	48
Maslenica	50
Pače Pita	52
Ružice	54
Jabukovača	56
Filovane Paprike	58
Pirimčlije	60
Japrak Sarma	62
Sarma	64
Sogani	66
Riblja Čorba	68
Riba	70
Triestino	72
Natur Šnicla	74
Banjalučka Šnicla	76
Čuftice	78
Salata od Mrkve	80
Mahune	82
Tuzla Pile	84
Pile sa Rižom	86
Patka i Omać	88
Dolma	90
Šilčići sa Bamijom	92
Begova Čorba	94
Bamija	96
Bosanski Lonac	98
Gulaš	100
Grah	102
Klepe	104
Medeno Meso	106
Ripa	108
Trahana	110
Ćevapi	112
Pljeskavica	114
Šiš Ćevap	116
Pašteta	118

Contents

Capsicum and Eggplant Relish	6
Pepper Butter	8
Leek and Eggs	10
Nana's Potatoes	12
Stuffed Peppers	14
Baked Peppers	16
Polenta	18
Bread	20
Bread Rolls with Onion	22
Turkish Bread	24
Soda Bread	26
Fried Bread Rolls	28
Flat Pudding Dessert	30
Flat Cream Pudding	32
Garlic Bread Pudding	34
"Yorkshire" Puddings	36
Filo Pastry	38
Filo Pastry with Mince	40
Filo Pastry Pockets	42
Spinach Filo	44
Potato Pastry	46
Pumpkin Pastry	48
Butter Filo Pastry	50
Parchment Pie	52
Baklava Roses	54
Apple Pie	56
Stuffed Capsicums	58
Meatballs	60
Vine Leaf Sarma	62
Stuffed Cabbage Rolls	64
Stuffed Onions	66
Fish Soup	68
Fish	70
Garlic Sauce	72
Schnitzel	74
Banja Luka Schnitzel	76
Meatballs in Sauce	78
Carrot Salad	80
Broadbeans	82
Salt Roast Chicken	84
Roast Chicken Pilav	86
Roast Duck Linguine	88
Bread and Rice Casserole	90
Meat Skewers with Okra	92
The Sultan's Soup	94
Okra	96
Bosnian Stew Pot	98
Goulash	100
Bean Soup	102
Dumplings	104
Honeyed Meat	106
Swedes	108
Sourdough Soup	110
Skinless Sausage	112
Burger Pattie	114
Skewered Ćevap	116
Pâté	118

Sir	120	Ricotta Cheese	120
Siriluk	122	Spring Onion Dip	122
Budimka	124	Roast Pumpkin	124
Griz	126	Semolina Pudding	126
Halva	128	Shortbread Rounds	128
Jabuke u Šlafruku	130	Apple Fritters	130
Kadaif	132	Kadaif Cake	132
Kahva i Šećer	134	Coffee and Sugar	134
Šape	136	Shortbread	136
Sutlije	138	Rice Pudding	138
Tufahije	140	Stuffed Apples	140
Hurmašice	142	Shortbread in Syrup	142
Palačinke	144	Crêpés	144

Mostar is one of the jewels of the Bosnian crown. Awash in starlight, and sleepy at dawn, it is a stop on all Bosnian culinary journeys.

AJVAR
CAPSICUM AND EGGPLANT RELISH

 10 minutes    3 hours

....

5kg Red Peppers
2kg Eggplant
Chilli Powder (to taste)
Salt (to taste)
Sugar (to taste)

....

Roast the capsicum and eggplant, preferably over coals. Set aside and allow to cool. Peel the vegetables, making sure to remove all the skin. Chop (manually or in a food processor) roughly.

Keep the juices and cook in large pot, adding salt and sugar to taste. There are often many variants to this dish, you can add chilli although the best hot ajvar comes from using a mixture of hot capsicums.

Keep cooking and stirring at a medium heat until there is no liquid left.

If you add some oil, it will speed up the cooking process and get you faster to the "no liquid" consistency. I usually don't.

The brilliant thing about ajvar is that it is so much more than a dip. If you choose to preserve it in small jars, much like any other relish, it works as a thickener for most soups and stews. I often use it as a pizza base or as an addition to salsa.

You can experiment with the ratio of the above.
This is a great camping dish and you can get the whole family involved. Don't forget to take jars.

Give it a shot by experimenting with different types of eggplant and capsicum.

The very best of camping ajvar was a mix of very sweet flavours given a beautiful char by the barbecue.

Ajvar on toast with 3 types of Chilli butter. Experiment with different chillis to get the right colour, flavour, and heat.

PUTER SA BIBEROM
PEPPER BUTTER

 5 minutes    20 minutes

250g Softened Butter
50g Peppercorns
Salt (to taste)

Grind the peppercorns.

Allow the butter to soften and then mix through the peppercorns, reserving a small portion for garnish.
Salt the mixture and confirm the taste is suitable.
Roll into little balls and then roll those balls in the ground peppercorns.

I love this very simple recipe as it was my grandmother's favourite. Nana would often call us into the kitchen, the butter melting on the hot bread, the slice already salted and peppered. "Whatever you are doing can wait, bread doesn't stay warm forever!".

During the war, I met a lot of old grandmothers from a lot of different parts of the Balkans, and each of them attempted to feed me. In Travnik, half frozen from the snow, an old grandmother ushered me into her house and gave me homemade warm bread with vegetable shortening, sprinkled with caster sugar. The recipe doesn't really match our modern lifestyle, but every time I see fairy-bread at a children's party in Australia, I remember the old Eba from Travnik.

Butter balls with red peppercorns served with two types of bread rolls.

ČILBUR

LEEK AND EGGS

 15 minutes   20 minutes

3 Free range eggs
½ a Leek
1 Tbsp Olive oil
1 Tsp Salt
Pepper (to taste)

Chop the leek, discarding the outside and green portions. If your leek is young, you should be able to simply sweat the chopped leek the same as you would an onion.

If the leek feels a bit tough, you can steam (or blanch it), before frying.

On a little bit of olive oil, fry the chopped leeks until golden. Reserve half.

Whip the eggs, pour over the leek and stir until cooked. Serve on crunchy toast and garnish with the reserved leek.

There are some exciting variations of this dish; you can exchange or add onions instead of leeks, and also include beef mince. At our house, this has always been a favourite for breakfast and matches beautifully with a runny fried egg.

Leek and egg salad on crunchy sourdough toast.

NANINI KROMPIRČIĆI
NANA'S POTATOES

 10 minutes   30 minutes

4 Cups Cubed Potatoes
1 Cup Cream
100g Butter
Spinach and Beetroot Leaves
Salt (to taste)

Wash and cube the potatoes. I like to use three different types as they will fry up differently and give you a variety of colour and textures, despite being equal in size.

The size should roughly be about 1cm cubed. My grandmother and I always disagreed whether the potatoes for this dish needed to be peeled. Use your own judgement. (Don't peel them.)

Fry the cubed potatoes on a knob of butter until soft and golden. Salt to your own taste and add the cream. Serve immediately in the hot dish as this will keep cooking the cream.

Add some spinach and beetroot leaves for colour.

Sweet potato is the best variant for this recipe.

We don't get sweet potato in Bosnia, so it was quite a treat.

Try this dish with both white and purple varieties, as they taste like chestnuts.

Nana's potatoes, drenched in cream, with beetroot and spinach leaves.

PUNJENE PAPRIKE
STUFFED PEPPERS

 10 minutes   30 minutes

3 small Capsicums
1 Potato
1 Tsp of Vegeta
3 Tbsp Olive Oil
1 Tsp Chilli Powder

Open the capsicum at the top leaving a little hat for it. Brush the inside and outside of the capsicum with the olive oil. I use infused olive oils for this dish such as truffle, rosemary, or garlic, to create depth.

Peel and slice finely on a mandolin (or chop) the potato. Traditionally, the potatoes would be cubed, as with most Bosnian dishes. Slicing them finely gives the same flavour but uses less potato and cooks the dish faster.

Dust the potatoes with Vegeta, and drizzle with the remaining oil.

Stuff the peppers and then place the little hat on, this will allow the potato to partially steam. Cook until the potatoes are soft and the peppers are charred. Sprinkle the chilli powder on top once cooked.

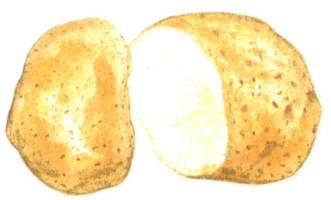

Baked Dolma peppers stuffed with potato, topped with sour cream.

PEČENE PAPRIKE
BAKED PEPPERS

 15 minutes    20 minutes

4 Large Peppers
4 Cloves Garlic
1 Cup Cream
Salt (to taste)

Wash and dry the peppers, and place them in a traditional tevsija; a deep baking dish.

Bake the peppers at 200°C for 20 minutes or until soft.

Chop or grate the garlic finely and mix in the cream and salt. Add the cream to the peppers and return the dish to the oven.

This is great side to any main, but works best with dry meats like turkey.

If you are feeling adventurous, add a few hot peppers. The baking intensifies the flavour and give this dish an amazing kick.

Use any leftovers for pizza or omelettes.

Roast capsicums with cream and garlic.

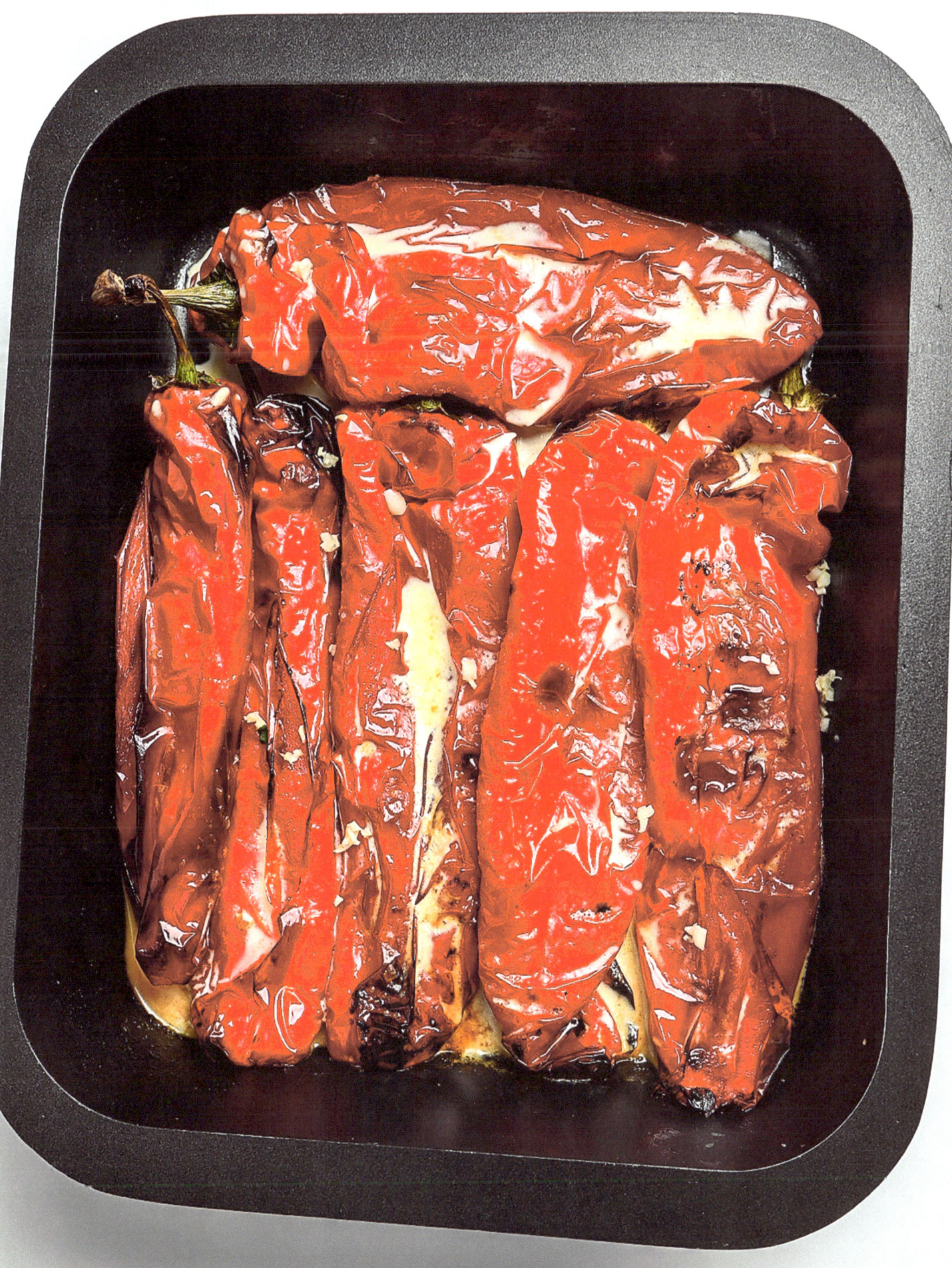

PURA
POLENTA

 3 minutes   20 minutes

3 Cups Water
1 Cup Polenta
50g Butter
1 Onion

1 Tbsp Sweet Paprika
1 Tbsp Salt
1/3 Cup Ricotta

Add the salt to the water and bring to the boil. One spoonful at time, add the polenta into the mixture, stirring as you go. If the mixture is too thick too quickly, add more water, so that you have enough time to cook the polenta properly. You will know that it is cooked when it does not taste floury. This dish will fight back, so be careful and wear long sleeves.

Once the polenta is cooked and thick, pull it aside to cool. In a little skillet, melt the butter and add the paprika, allow it to burn just a little bit and for the butter to separate. Spoon the polenta into the skillet and serve with a soft cheese (or sour cream) and raw onion.

The onion is what makes the dish. Nana always insisted that you must step on the onion to remove the bitterness, rather than chopping it. If you are serving guests, I recommend you squash your onion with a frying pan.

Polenta with butter, paprika, onion, and cheese.

SOMUN
BREAD

 3 hours   45 minutes

5 Cups Plain Flour
2½ Cups Warm Water
½ Cup Oil
1 Tbsp Sugar
1 Tbsp Salt
1 Tbsp Dry Yeast

Place the sugar, dry yeast, and 1 cup of warm water in a dish to activate and feed the yeast. Sift the flour and place in a large bowl. Add the salt around the edge of the flour. Make a little well in the middle of the bowl and place the sugar and yeast mixture in the well.

Gently mix the ingredients from the inside out, adding slowly more and more of the flour. Add the rest of the warm water and the oil. Eventually, start mixing in the salt from the edges in. Once all is well mixed, leave the dough to prove for 2 hours.

Then, knead the dough again and leave it to rise a second time. This is the standard dough mixture we refer to in this book. The baking method is what makes each bread a little bit different.

Baking it in a normal pan produces a bread with solid crumb and a thin crust, perfect for buttering. I really enjoy a crunchy bread and use the cast iron pot method to get a decent crust.

Preheat your oven and your cast iron pot, as hot as you can. Sprinkle the cast iron pot with flour and place the dough inside. Cut lines in the dough so that it does not burst, sprinkle some flour on the top, and shut the lid. Bake at the hottest your oven will go for about 25 minutes.

Crunchy bread baked in a cast iron pot. The cast iron pot method will make any oven into a traditional Bosnian bell oven.

KIFLICE SA LUKOM
BREAD ROLLS WITH ONION

 3 hours    35 minutes

Bread Mix (page 20)   1 Tsp Sugar
4 Onions   1 Tsp Salt
2 Egg Yolks   Optional Garnish
1 Tbsp Olive Oil

For the dough, see bread recipe on page 20.

To make the filling, chop or grate the onions.

In non stick frying pan, heat up the oil, and add the chopped onions. Add the salt and sugar and fry the onions until caramelised and delicious. Allow to cool.

Roll the dough to about ½ cm thickness and into a large circular shape. Cut wedges into the dough from the outside in, making very steep and thin pyramids.

On the outer edge, spoon a little bit of the onion mixture and then spread towards the inside, stopping well before the middle. Roll each wedge into a crescent shape so that the middle is the thickest.

Place each roll onto a lined baking tray and brush with egg yolk. Sprinkle with your chosen garnish (Sesame, rock salt, poppy seed, or caraway seed) and bake at 190° Celsius until golden brown.

There is a similar dish pictured opposite page 8 made with ajvar. The method also works with cocktail frankfurters, jam, cheese, or any other condiment.

Bread rolls with onion.

LEPINE

TURKISH BREAD

 2 hours    7 minutes

5 Cups Plain Flour
3 Cups Water
⅓ Cup Oil
2 Tbsp Sugar
1 Tbsp Yeast
1 Tbsp Salt

Mix all the ingredients together. Allow plenty time for the dough to rise. Dust your work surface with flour, then separate the mixture into dough balls the size of your palms. Knead them individually adding more flour as needed. Preheat your oven to 350° Celsius.

Roll out the balls until they are the size and thickness of your hand. They should all be roughly uniform. The typical Bosnian lepina is round.

Using a knife and a thin cloth gently press lines into the lepina so you get a diamond pattern forming. Be careful not to cut or score the dough. Allow the dough to rise once again.

Dust your baking tray with flour or with wheat rusk, place the lepine on the tray and let the lepine rest again for 10-15 minutes. Bake at the hottest temperature your oven will get to.

Try using a cookie sheet without edges to ensure that there is the least amount of steam being trapped by the edges of the baking tray.

They should be golden on top, some burn spots are acceptable at that temperature, the dough should have risen in the oven at least double in height.

Cool your lepine on a cooling rack.

The Sebilj in Sarajevo is a fountain, built in 1753.

If you stand on the steps and look towards town, as far as the eye can see, there are different eateries serving some of the best lepine.

Tray of Lepine.

POGAČA
SODA BREAD

 20 minutes    30 minutes

5 Cups Flour
1½ Cups Sparkling Water
1 Cup Plain Yogurt
1 Tbsp Baking powder
1 Tbsp Salt

This soda bread does not need to prove or rise. It will be flat, dense, with a strong crumb and wonderful with stews. The yogurt and sparkling water help the bread leaven.

Combine the ingredients and knead the bread until it forms a ball in your hand. If you leave it a bit runnier than normal dough, it will be a bit softer.

Bake for 30 minutes at 180° Celsius.

When I was about four, Nana invited all her friends to a lunch to watch me bake soda bread. She placed a large white table cloth on the floor and sat me in her lap, the ingredients around us as if some sacred rite was about to be performed. Slowly, she explained the process to me, and had me place each ingredient in the large bowl.

The ladies called out suggestions. I kneaded the bread (and made a spectacular mess).

While the bread baked, the ladies had coffee and Nana made the rest of our meal. I served the soda bread to the women in the room, awash in praise and joy.

If you want your little ones to enjoy cooking, and they are not shy, I recommend the bread-party method as a way of forming life long happy associations.

Try a bread and butter pudding made with bone broth, butter, and a heaping of pepper. If that is too much effort, I typically crumb soda bread instead of croûtons in most soups.

UŠTIPAK

FRIED BREAD ROLLS

 10 minutes    10 minutes

5 Cups Flour
1 Cup Yogurt
1 Cup Milk
1 Cup Sparkling Water
1 Tbsp Baking Powder
1 Egg

1 Tbsp Salt
1 Tsp Sugar
1 Tsp Dry Yeast

Mix the ingredients until you get a doughy consistency. Separate into equal soft round balls. Heat oil in a deep frying pan.

You can check if it is the right temperature by dripping one drop of water into the mixture and listening for the sizzle. Place one round ball into the oil at a time. Expect that this will lower the temperature of your cooking oil, so go slowly. After a few minutes, turn the uštipak over. The more oil you use, the more even the colour and the rounder the shape.

Drip dry your uštipke (plurak of uštipak) on a plate with mounds of paper towel. Serve either as a savoury accompaniment to ajvar, siriluk, or with a stew.

If you make a batch that is slightly smaller, you will get a more crunchy ball, and you can dust them with icing sugar and drizzle with runny jam or maple syrup.

You could use the same bread recipe from page 22 to make uštipke, they will be softer in the middle and will have absorbed more oil. Both are an acceptable variant for an uštipak.

Typically we make uštipke in a rush; guests are arriving, it's breakfast time, there is some sort of bread related emergency. Using the above baking soda mixture, rather than the yeast mixture, simply means you do not have to wait for the bread to prove.

This is the old bridge in Mostar. Our first night there, my husband and I ordered the breadbasket.

Out came the most magnificent tray of different types of uštipak, as light and fluffy as clouds.

FILDŽANUŠA
FLAT PUDDING DESSERT

 10 minutes    35 minutes

2½ Cups Flour
1½ Cup Boiling Water
1 Cup Runny Apple Jam
1 Cup Room Temperature Water
1 Tsp Salt

Mix the apple jam and 1 cup of room temperature water and set aside. Mix the rest of the ingredients in a pan over the heat and keep mixing until the dough forms into a ball. Allow to cool slightly.

Flatten the mixture into a baking tray. Using a small cup (which is where the dish gets its name from) make the circular pattern in the dough. Bake for 20 minutes until golden and then pour the jam mixture over the top and cover.

If you do not have access to Bosnian apple jam, you can do this either with honey, golden syrup, or maple syrup.

For a modern take, cut the dough into rounds and serve as you would waffles or pancakes, with whipped cream, ground almonds, mint, and summer fruit.

Bosnian apple jam is easy enough to make. You need to juice 100kg of apples to get about 30-40L of apple juice. Or buy the apple juice and cook on a rolling boil for about 8 hours until it reduces.

Flat pudding dessert in the traditional tevsija.

KAŠIKAČA
FLAT CREAM PUDDING

 10 minutes   35 minutes

2½ Cups Flour
1½ Cups Boiling Water
1 Cup Cream
1 Tsp Salt

Sift the flour and salt into a large pan and add the boiling water. Cook the mixture over the heat and keep mixing until the dough forms into a ball. Allow to cool slightly.

Flatten the mixture into a baking tray. Using a large spoon make the circular pattern in the dough, this will allow for the cream to pool after baking. Bake for 20 minutes until golden and then pour the cream over the top and cover.

This dish is very suitable as an alternative to pizzas and garlic breads and is a great accompaniment to any meat or vegetable dish. Quite often it would be served sprinkled with ricotta cheese or siriluk at a brunch.

Each town and village in Bosnia has a different name for a large variety of the dishes we make. This flat cream pudding is named after the shape made by a regular soup spoon giving it its distinctive texture.

Flat cream pudding.

KLJUKUŠA
GARLIC BREAD PUDDING

 10 minutes  35 minutes

2½ Cups Flour
1½ Cups Boiling Water
1 Cup Cream
100g Butter
9 Cloves Garlic
1 Tsp Salt

In a large pot, bring 1½ cups of water to the boil and mix in the flour and salt. This should produce a ball that comes away from the pot. Allow to cool slightly and tap into small pancakes and then place into a tray to bake. When the mixture is golden brown, remove and again allow to cool so that you can tear it into small pieces.

Mix the butter, the chopped garlic, and the cream. Toss the golden nuggets through the cream mixture until evenly spread.

This makes a great entertaining dish and is a favourite amongst anyone who is a fan of garlic bread. I typically serve it accompanying a meaty main and a simple tomato salad. Very rarely are there leftovers, but they work brilliantly instead of croûtons in a soup or as a base for loaded fries.

I used to think of this dish as a reward for burnt fingertips from tearing the dough into pieces. A modern tip is to use a pizza knife to cut the dough into rough small squares before baking. This allows for easier tearing and less burns.

Make this dish whenever you feel like something decadent.

MUTUŠA

"YORKSHIRE" PUDDINGS

 10 minutes    20 minutes

2 Cups Flour
1 Cup Milk
1 Egg
1 Cup Cream
1 Tbsp Baking Powder
1 Tbsp salt

Other ingredients for toppings

Except for the cream, mix all the ingredients together until you get a mixture slightly thicker than that for pancakes. You can prepare the mixture in advance and leave it to rest the glutens.

Preheat your oven to 200° Celsius and prepare the other ingredients you would like to use. Decide if you are using your muffin tins or a baking dish. The muffin tins will need to be oiled while I recommend lining the baking tin.

The mini version works as a canapé, whilst I tend to make the pan slice version for family meals.

Pour the mixture into your dish and sprinkle the toppings, expecting that the dough will slightly raise to cover them.

Bake until golden and then pour the cream on top and return to the oven for five minutes.

This is my favourite versatile dish. There is an endless number of ingredients and options that could work together and can make the dish as light or as heavy as you want it. Great topping combinations to experiment with: mincemeat and onion, marinated chicken wings, cheese and spinach, capsicum and potato, plain with cream.

Shredded spinach and cheese can be mixed into the body of the dish to add to the texture.

The mini version works as a wonde-ful canapé.

JUFKA
FILO PASTRY

 2 hours  20 minutes

5 Cups Flour
2½ Cups of Water
½ Cup Oil
1 Tbsp Salt
Pinch of Dry Yeast

Mix the ingredients well and form into three equal shaped balls. Place the balls onto an oiled tray, oil the top, and wrap in clingfilm. They will need to rest for 1-2 hours. No more and no less.

You can put them in the freezer for a month and in the fridge for a week, but they will need to come to temperature slowly.

To roll out the filo pastry, use a dedicated table cloth and a long thin rolling pin (called oklagija). Dust the surface with flour and roll out, turning the dough as needed.

Once the dough is less than ½ cm in thickness, if you are new to filo pastry, put down the rolling pin, oil the dough, let it rest for a few minutes, and slowly, with your hands, pull the dough to stretch it further. Working first one corner, than the opposite, until the filo becomes almost transparent. Bosnian children grow up rolling out filo and can wave and twirl it like a flag. The key is not to be afraid of the pastry.

If it starts tearing, this is normal, at the beginning. Stop, take a deep breath, oil the pastry and let it rest for a few minutes. Keep going.

The dry yeast ingredient is a secret told to The Chef's wife, during the war, by an old grandmother who was worried that her family recipes would die out. I hope by including it here that a new generation of bakers will delight in her pastry.

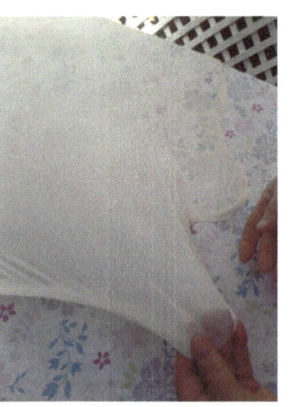

Jufka being rolled with a traditional oklagija (rolling pin).

BUREK

FILO PASTRY WITH MINCE

 30 minutes    30 minutes

500g Beef Mince
2 Onions
⅓ Cup Oil
Jufka (page 38)

1 Shredded Potato
1 Cup Cream
1 Tbsp Salt

You will need the recipe for jufke (page 38 or 250g of filo pastry). Roll out the jufka across a large dining room table on a white table cloth and use ⅓ of the oil to oil the sheet, or, if using store-bought, keep it under a damp towel and use aerosol oil spray. Finely chop the onions. Mix all the ingredients except for the oil and cream. As store bought pastry will bake quicker than homemade pastry, you should fry the mixture and cool it, if you are using the store bought pastry.

Sprinkle the mixture on the pastry at each edge and roll inwards so as to create a log. Then roll those logs into snail shapes and place on an oiled or lined baking tray. Oil the snails and bake for 25 minutes or until golden brown. Pour the cream over the top and then bake again for a further 5 minutes.

It is possible to do this dish in a variety of ways. Chopped beef, rather than mince, creates a sort of gravy that is divine. My favourite was made leftover barbecued steak that gave it a smoky profile.

The potato quantity can be adjusted and increased. Strictly speaking, the potato is not necessary, although it has textural benefits. Making these dishes is a professional calling; a type of specialised chef. The pastries are sold in specialised bakeries throughout Bosnia. The inclusion of one shredded potato was recommended to me by a professional baker in Prjedor, Bosnia whose family brought the recipe from Albania.

If you use half meat and half chopped potato, it is more noticeable and flavourful. Finally, the pastry can be layered, much like a lasagne, and then baked. Serve with fresh acidic vegetables or with pickles.

Burek, served with pickles.

MANTIJE
FILO PASTRY POCKETS

 30 minutes   40 minutes

300g Chicken meat
1 Large Onion
1 Tbsp Vegeta
1 Cup Cream
Olive Oil Spray
Jufka (page 38)

The recipe for jufke (page 38 or 250g of filo pastry). For the meat, chicken thigh or breast work best.

Preheat your oven to 180° Celsius.

Dice the chicken and onion and add the Vegeta. If you are using store bought filo pastry, cook the chicken/onion mixture, allow to cool, and then use it.

If you are making your own filo, the cooking time is increased, and the chicken will cook at the same time as your pastry.

Roll the pastry onto a clean white dedicated table cloth, oil with the aerosol oil, and slice into long sheets about 15cm long and 5 cm wide. Try to make each sheet the same size. Don't stress if there are small breaks in the pastry.

Spoon the chicken mixture onto the pastry and roll into shapes the size of your two thumbs in width.

Place the first row of mantije into a lined baking tray as normal. Place the second row (and all other rows) as if you were tiling a roof, ensuring that they overlap.

Bake for 30-35 minutes until golden brown and the chicken is cooked through. Pour the cream on top, and bake for a further five minutes.

As a young lad, our Chef competed at the culinary games and won Bronze. His winning dish; this recipe for mantije.

(We forgive him for not coming first as Nana won Gold, and his boss won Silver.)

ZELJANICA

SPINACH FILO

 30 minutes    25 minutes

500g Spinach
3 Eggs
1kg Ricotta
Jufka (page 38)
1 Cup Cream
4 Tbsp White Ground Pepper

2 Tbsp Salt

Wash each leaf individually and dry. Slice finely, and reserve the stalks. Add in the eggs, cheese, salt and half the pepper. I like to use my own home made ricotta for this dish, although any mixture of soft cheeses, such as a dry curd, or a cottage cheese, should work.

If you want to be sneaky, you can grate 200g of Bulgarian or Persian feta into the cheese mixture that will add an amazing richness (and the calories).

The trick with zeljanica is in the white pepper.

Roll out your pastry and sprinkle the remaining pepper on the pastry. Then, spoon on the spinach mixture, ensuring that you do not miss the edges. If your mixture is too wet, this will create trouble, so work quickly and ensure that you have drained your cheese if need be.

Bake for 20-25 minutes at medium heat, and once golden, either leave crispy or sprinkle some water to soften the filo.

My grandmother (and mother) are enamoured with a soup made entirely out of the leftover chopped spinach stalks and cooked rice. If you are so inclined, use the reserved stalks with four cups of water and 1 cup of rice, for an interesting congee like soup.

To make sirnica (a cheese pastry without the spinach) simply exclude the spinach in the above recipe.

Spinach swirls.

KROMPIRUŠA
POTATO PASTRY

 30 minutes   40 minutes

6 Potatoes
2 Onions
2 Tbsp Vegeta
Jufka (page 38)
2 Tbsp Pepper
⅓ Cup Oil

You will need the recipe for jufke (page 38 or 250g of filo pastry). Peel and cube the potatoes and the onions. If you are using dried filo, you must cook the potatoes and onions first. It is not common to do so if you are working with your own home made pastry, although, the step can provide for a much softer potato, almost like a mashed potato, which is brilliant. Add the pepper, Vegeta, and half the oil to the potatoes.

Roll out the pastry on a large table and cut in half. Spread the mixture in a thick line along the edge of the table on each portion of the pastry. Drizzle again with oil and, sprinkle the cracked pepper all over the pastry. This will complete the flavour profile of the dish. It is possible to also sprinkle hot chilli at this point, although unnecessary. Then, roll the pastry inwards into logs and form into snails (or spirals).

Some people sprinkle the dish with either hot water or cream when it is done baking. I typically don't as I prefer it crunchy. Once you are used to making your own pita, you will quickly have your own thoughts on the matter, too.

This dish is very common and is usually served with yogurt or sauerkraut, something acidic to break through the richness of the potato.

The best version I ever had was with potatoes that had been partially baked on open flame.

Cooled, chopped, and used in the pastry the next day.

Potato pastry rounds with the usual suspects.

The Lost Chef - Page 46

MASIRAČA
PUMPKIN PASTRY

 30 minutes   30 minutes

Jufka (page 38)
1 Large Pumpkin
2 Tbsp Olive Oil
1 Tbsp Vegeta
1 Cup Cream

The recipe for jufke is to be used or 250g of filo pastry.

The large pumpkin (or large zucchini) needs to provide five cups of diced flesh

Cube the pumpkin and shred or chop the onion. Add the oil and Vegeta to the mixture. If you are using a firmer pumpkin or are using store bought pastry, it is always best to fry it in some olive oil first, with the onion, let it cool, and then use that mixture. If you have managed to find the right kind of overgrown zucchini, or have planted your own, then there is no need to fry the mixture.

As with all pita, roll out the pastry across the table on a cloth and spread the mixture on both sides of the table. Slice in the middle, and roll the mixture forward to create two large logs. You can either create small snails as in the previous recipes or a large snail, as seen here.

Bake for 25-30 minutes or until golden brown. If you want a crunchy filo (or simply to keep the dish vegan), then do not pour the cream on top.

This dish works brilliantly if you have guests who are either vegan or vegetarian.

I typically serve it as meza with sliced meat if we have a mixed group.

Pumpkin pastry with cucumber on a traditional Bosnian rug.

MASLENICA
BUTTER FILO PASTRY

 30 minutes   35 minutes

250g Butter
1 Cup Cream
Jufka (page 38)
Salt (to taste)

I do not recommend you bake this with store bought filo, it is one of the few dishes that really relies on your ability to work with the pastry while it is wet.

Preheat your oven to 200° Celsius.

Roll out the filo pastry and drizzle each sheet generously with the butter and cream mixture. Then, tuck in the edges, creating little pockets of air and place into your tray as sheets. Repeat this for all the layers, till you have about 5-8cm in height for your maslenica. Bake in the oven for 25 minutes or until golden brown. There is no need to pour cream over the top, the maslenica is meant to be crunchy and flaky.

This dish works much like a croissant, great with chocolate and jam, brilliant for a sandwich or to tuck into a bit of soup, or as simple and humble on its own.

If you are planning on using your maslenica as a savory dish, a great variant is to sprinkle finely chopped capsicum or hot paprika on the sheets of pastry at the same time as the cream. Serve that with a hearty bean stew or as a base for a roast chicken.

Maslenica with apple jam.

PAČE PITA
PARCHMENT PIE

 50 minutes    30 minutes

3 Cups Shredded Chicken
3 Cups Chicken Stock
1 Cup Cream
Jufka (page 38)

Roll the filo pastry and cut into sheets the size of your baking dish. Then, on a hot stone tray or a shallow frying pan, cook the pastry so that it is crunchy. Expect small burn marks, these are common. Set the pastry aside to cool.

At the bottom, place two slices of pastry, then a layer of the cooked meat and a little bit of the chicken stock, then same for each additional layer, finishing with the pastry.

Slice the mixture and then add the rest of the chicken stock slowly. Bake for half an hour at 180° Celsius until the top has browned. Add the 1 cup of cream and return to the oven for a further five minutes.

Depending on your dish, it is perfectly reasonable to serve either in slices, wedges, or cubes. This dish depends on a good flavourful salad with high acidity.

For added complexity you can make this dish with duck meat and stock.

The carrot salad is a punchy accompaniment.

My translation is unfair to the dish. Whilst parchment is what the baked filo resembles, the original name suggests it was most likely made with duck rather than chicken.

RUŽICE
BAKLAVA ROSES

 30 minutes    1 hour

Jufka (page 38)
1kg Ground Walnuts
200g Caster Sugar
250g Unsalted Butter
1 Tbsp Vanilla Paste
2 Lemons

1kg Sugar
1 Litre Water

This dish is a Baklava shaped as a rose. A further variant is to replace the walnuts with almonds and hazelnuts in equal parts. If you are rolling out your filo pastry, you will need many working surfaces for the pastry to dry. My recommendation is that you kick everyone out of your house and once the pastry has been rolled, place the sheets onto all available surfaces to dry.

Sprinkle your pastry with corn flour to help it dry and go make a cup of coffee. Place the ground walnuts, vanilla paste, 2 lemon's worth of zest, the caster sugar into a bowl and mix well.

Cut the sheets into the length and size of your baking dish.

The first three sheets of filo only a little sprinkle of walnut mixture, the fourth layer needs to be sprayed with melted butter, and covered in the walnut mixture. Repeat this four times, so that the pastry layers are about $1^{1}/_{2}$ cm tall. Then, roll the pastry into a tight log that should be about 6cm in diameter. Cut the logs into 3cm slices and place tightly into the tray. Bake the dish for 25 minutes or until golden.

Prepare the 1kg of sugar and 1 litre of water mixture and bring to the boil. Add the wedges of lemon and stir for 10 minutes. Then, pour the syrup over the dish and cover to allow it to soak.

Baklava is a similar recipe but the layers are stacked differently.

Much like parchment pie, they are layered and then cut into shape. Whilst you don't have to use a ruler, it helps.

Roses served on apple slices with almond shavings.

JABUKOVAČA

APPLE PIE

 30 minutes   30 minutes

Jufka (page 38)
500g Apples
100g Butter
3 Tbsp Vanilla Sugar
1 Tbsp Cinnamon
200g Sugar

2 Cups Water
1 Wedge Lemon

I always prefer this recipe, as with any using pastry, made with homemade filo pastry. If you are in a rush or determined to avoid covering your entire kitchen in flour, then store bought filo works fine. Keep the store bought filo under a damp cloth and spray with aerosol vegetable oil to moisten it while using.

Shred the apples and fry them gently in butter. Add the vanilla sugar and ground cinnamon to the mixture and allow to cool.

Roll out your pastry and sprinkle the apple mixture. Roll the mixture into thin logs, and then place into a baking dish. Spray with oil and bake at 180 degrees for 25 minutes.

While this is baking, boil the remaining sugar, water, and lemon, until a simple syrup is formed. Once the apple pastry is golden, remove from the oven, slice into pockets, and pour over the sugar syrup. Allow the pastry to soak up the syrup before serving. The syrup is popular in a lot of Bosnian desserts. You could not include it in this dish if you sought a crunchier pastry.

Apple pie served with fresh apple.

FILOVANE PAPRIKE
STUFFED CAPSICUMS

 30 minutes    1 hour

8 Small Capsicums
500g Beef Mince
1 Cup Rice
1 Tbsp Vegeta
1 Tbsp Black Pepper
2 Tbsp Tomato Paste

Water to Cover
Paprika to Garnish

Wash, dry, and remove the lids of the capsicums. Reserve the lids. The red capsicums tend to be sweeter, but the yellow are a personal favourite. In a bowl mix the beef, rice, Vegeta, black pepper. This forms the stuffing. Prepare a large pot for the capsicums, or a very deep casserole dish, by placing the lids at the bottom of the pot. Then, stuff each capsicum with a little bit of the mixture and place it, top up, into the pot. Mix the tomato paste with a little bit of water, and pour over the top. Then, pour enough water to cover the capsicums and bring them to the boil.

Once boiling, reduce the temperature to a gentle simmer and leave cooking for 1 hour. If you are using a casserole dish, do the same, cover tightly with baking paper and aluminium foil, and bake in the oven in the same manner.

The dish is best served with mash or scalloped potato or as seen here with an accompaniment of other stuffed vegetables. These dishes work really well with home style buffets when you are feeding a large group of people. To individualise them, you could bake them in ramekins or little clay pots and serve with cream. Garnish with the paprika.

Stuffed capsicums, served here with meatballs and stuffed onions on a soft lepina.

PIRIMČLIJE
MEATBALLS

 10 minutes    1 hour

500g Beef Mince
1 Cup Rice
1 Tbsp Vegeta
1 Tbsp Black Pepper
2 Tbsp Tomato Paste
½ Cup Oil

2 Tbsp Flour
1 Cup Water
1 Tbsp Hot Paprika

A pir is a banquet, and these rice meatballs are traditionally served as part of large banquets with a variety of dry or stewed dishes, hence the name. The mixture is similar to that used to stuff various vegetables throughout the Balkans and every family has its own little trick.

Mix the beef, rice, Vegeta and black pepper and then create small even balls. You should be able to get exactly 40 from this mixture. Place them in a casserole dish or a pot, sprinkle the paprika, and cover with water. Allow the water to reduce.

In a separate dish, heat up the oil and add the flour. Cook the flour till it is golden, and then carefully add in the tomato paste and water. This sauce is often added to many Bosnian dishes to thicken them, and you can decide if you would like to add it to your stews or not. Most modern cooking avoids the sauce as it is quite rich and decadent.

Add the sauce to the dish, stir gently. If you are using a casserole dish, and the tops of your meatballs are not getting enough water, flip them gently. They should simmer for about 40 minutes until cooked.

Rice and beef meatballs served in rec' sauce.

JAPRAK SARMA

VINE LEAF SARMA

 10 minutes    3 hours

40 Vine Leaves
500g Beef Mince
1 Cup Rice
2 Tbsp Tomato Paste
1 Tbsp Vegeta
1 Tbsp Black Pepper

Water to cover
1 Tbsp Paprika

For this dish you should choose young vine leaves, slightly bigger than the palm of your hand (not the fingers). If they are fresh, first place them in hot water with some lemon and salt, and bring to the boil. Remove from the boil and set aside to cool.

If you are picking your own vine leaves either do the above, or if you will eat them later, freeze them. This will change the leaf and they will not need boiling. Instead, thaw them in lukewarm water with lemon and salt. If the leaves are older, carefully remove the stalk from the middle.

Mix the beef, rice, Vegeta, black pepper, and paprika, into a mixture.

Carefully, place 1tbs or so of the mixture in the middle of your vine leaf and wrap them gently, tucking in the edges. Place them carefully in the tray, cover with water and the tomato paste, bring to the boil, then reduce and cook for 2 hours or until vine leaves are soft.

You can leave them in their stew, create the sauce mentioned in the previous recipe, or serve them individually on a bed of roast potatoes.

Vine leaf sarma with cheese and cream.

SARMA
STUFFED CABBAGE ROLLS

 35 minutes    1 hour

40 Sauerkraut Leaves
500g Beef mince
1 Cup Rice
1 Tbsp Vegeta
1 Tbsp Black Pepper
2 Tbsp Tomato Paste

Water to Cover
1 Tbsp Paprika

Boil the sauerkraut leaves and then take them out of the hot water to cool. Remove the middle stalks and aim for a leaf the size of your hand.

Mix the beef, rice, Vegeta, and black pepper, and spoon out equal portions on the cabbage leaves, wrapping them and tucking in the corners.

Any leftover bits of cabbage can go on the bottom of the pot. Then, layer the cabbage rolls. Sprinkle the paprika, mix the water and the tomato paste and cover the rolls in the pot with the liquid.

Cook for 2-3 hours, until the cabbage leaves are soft.
Traditionally, this dish would also be thickened with sauce mentioned in the previous recipes. It is not necessary, although delicious and useful for added decadence. I sometimes prefer to serve this dish on mashed potato and always with either sour cream or cream.

It is also interesting to serve the dish in reverse. In a deep ramekin, pile the cabbage rolls at the bottom and cover with mashed potato, creating dimples as you go, then some yellow cheese, and return to the oven to crisp up the top.

Rows of sarma served with chilli butter.

SOGANI

STUFFED ONIONS

 40 minutes    1 hour

40 Onion Rounds
500g Beef Mince
1 Cup Rice
1 Tbsp Vegeta
1 Tbsp Black Pepper
2 Tbsp Tomato Paste

Water to Cover
1 Tbsp Paprika

You will need 3-6 equally sized brown onions, depending on how good you are at extracting the insides and how thick the onions are. Peel them, careful not to remove the stump at the bottom, slice vertically from the center point to the edge, and then boil them for 15 minutes. This will soften the onion and make it workable.

Once the onions have cooled, remove the stumps, and separate out the layers. Carefully maintain the curvature of the onion. Pick your best 40.

Mix the mince, rice, Vegeta, black pepper and carefully stuff the onions, aiming for them to all be the same size. The leftover onion can be placed on the bottom of the dish and does not need to be stuffed. If you are serving a multitude of dishes, then chop the leftover onion and caramelise them, so that they can form a sauce or relish.

Sprinkle with paprika, mix in the water and tomato sauce, and then bring to the boil. Allow the dish to simmer for 1 hour with the lid on. I do not recommend you thicken the dish too much with the sauce mentioned in the previous pages. The onions look very delicate as they are, and group beautifully in a deep dish as a simple starter or, if you serve them in the casserole, as a hearty main.

Stuffed onions are a staple during Ramadan, where we typically make the extra effort to remember our traditional cooking and spend time reconnecting with our communities. They are always sure to impress.

RIBLJA ČORBA

FISH SOUP

 15 minutes    1 hour

900g Fish
3 Onions
4 Tbsp Tomato Paste
3 Tbsp Pepper
2 Tbsp Vegeta
1 Tbsp Olive Oil

2 Bay Leaves
1 Tbsp Sugar
Salt (to taste)
Sugar (to taste)

For this dish we typically use at least three types of fish with variations of dry and oily. Cod and catfish are popular in Bosnia, although I have made this dish with salmon, tuna, or snapper, and they are all equally as delicious. The variety of fish is what gives its depth of flavour. You need about 300g of each fish (aim for just under a kilo in total).

Once you have cleaned the fish, sprinkle it with Vegeta, pepper, and hot paprika.

Sweat the chopped onions on some olive oil, add the tomato paste, and then add sugar to taste. You may or may not need the whole spoonful, so start slowly. It is there to break the acidity of the dish.

Gently add the fish and cover it with water. Bring the dish to the boil and then reduce to a simmer for about 50 minutes. Serve with crunchy bread and lemon.

This soup was typically made at camping sites, when whole families would go down to the river to fish for the weekend. My parents owned a houseboat on the Sava and this was the standard lunch of those adventures.

RIBA
FISH

 10 minutes    25 minutes

1 Large Fish
1 Bunch Parsley
5 Cloves Garlic
2 Tbsp Rock Salt
1 Bunch Spring Onion
2 Lemons

Bosnia is mostly landlocked, although if you have a chance to go down to our coastline on the Adriatic, it is spectacular.

Our rivers are fierce, beautiful, and life giving. Typically most of the fish that we eat is freshwater and people like my dad would catch them freehand in the Sava.

When The Chef held his restaurant in Bosnia, we had a large pool at the front of the property, nestled amongst my grandfather's vineyards, where you could catch your own fish and then bring it to the kitchen to have it prepared for you.

Make a quick marinade for the fish with rock salt, plenty of oil, and bunches of parsley. Cover the fish with the marinade, leaving plenty to baste the fish. Bring your BBQ to a high temperature and place your fish on there. Turn the fish every five minutes, basting generously, and cook for about 25 minutes.

I like to serve it on spring onion, although any aromatic herbs will do.

Include plenty of lemon and lime and the recipe for Triestino on the next page.

Barbecued fish, served with triestino sauce, lemon slices, and spring onion.

TRIESTINO
GARLIC SAUCE

 10 minutes

10 Cloves Garlic
2 Bunches Parsley
2 Cups Olive Oil
1 Pinch Salt
1 Lemon

Peel 10 cloves of garlic, salt them, and leave them to rest.

Place two cups of oil in a large bowl and add to that the two bunches of finely chopped broad leaf parsley.
Finely chop the garlic and add to the mixture. Stir through.

Apply lovingly to all seafood, remembering to drizzle with lemon at the end.

As a child I thought this was a family recipe, some sort of secret. Certainly my grandmother, mother, and my uncle all made it and none of the other adults did. The Chef tells me it's a standard recipe, popular amongst the chefs he studied with, and common enough that it should be considered a staple.

I've served it a few times as a dipping sauce as an alternative to garlic bread.

NATUR ŠNICLA
SCHNITZEL

 10 minutes   20 minutes

3 Veal Schnitzel
½ Cup Oil
2 Tbsp Flour
2 Tbsp Water
1 Tbsp Vegeta

Beat the schnitzels with a hammer until tenderised. Cover with Vegeta.

Place the flour on a plate and then dab the schnitzels on one side in the flour.

Place the floured side down in a pan with the sizzling hot oil. After 90 seconds, that side should be cooked. Flip to the other side and cook for a further 90 seconds. Then, add the two tablespoons of water to create a sauce and allow to thicken.

When The Chef was at culinary school, his moniker was Šnicla (the Bosnian word for schnitzel) as it was his favourite dish. Served with a crunchy bruschetta, or a salad and fries, it has always been a family favourite, and very much my go-to dish in any restaurant.

During the war mum would draw plates for us, and tell us to draw and colour our favourite meals.

On most days, I drew mashed potato and schnitzels, with runny gravy. A friend once asked me why I spent my childhood drawing food. I pretended to confess to having been a foodie at seven. Honestly, it was a war; I was hungry.

BANJALUČKA ŠNICLA

BANJA LUKA SCHNITZEL

 10 minutes    20 minutes

Natur Schnitzel (page 74)
3 Slices Trappist Cheese
3 Slices Cured Beef

The Chef was born in Banja Luka, which is an old castle town in the northern part of Bosnia. The Banja Luka schnitzel includes a slice of a firm yellow cheese made by the Trappist monks.

My husband and I visited the Trappist monastery in chase of the perfect grilling cheese, and found it nestled in the woods a few kilometers out of the town centre.

The hunt for the Banja Luka schnitzel then took us to Novoselija, where my Nana was born, and to the dance-hall (now a restaurant) where The Chef used to go dancing as a youth. There they served us the schnitzel, with fine slices of smoked meat (suho meso) and grilled Trappist Cheese.

It is the same recipe as the Natur Schnitzel with a few additions.

If you cannot find suho meso (most countries require the addition of nitrates for cured meats to be food safe so we will not include the traditional recipe herein), Italian bresaola is also a lovely substitute, as it is also an air dried beef, or smoked turkey breast. I once had a variant with home cured venison that was spectacular.

Simply make the schnitzel, add your slices of meat, place slices of the Trappist cheese (and if none is available, Edam is a fine substitute) and grill for 7 minutes.

ČUFTICE
MEATBALLS IN SAUCE

 10 minutes    1 hour

500g Beef Mince
1 Cup Cream
1 Cup Flour
½ Cup Oil
1 Egg
2 Tbsp Vegeta

2 Tbsp Paprika
1 Tbsp Parsley

Mix the beef, Vegeta, half the paprika, half the parsley, and egg.

Work the mixture with your hands, much like you would a dough, until it is sticky and comes away easily from the bowl.

Make the balls and roll them in the flour. This mixture should allow you to make exactly 40 meatballs.

Heat a shallow pan with oil, fry the meatballs, once they are brown, add 1 cup cream and sweet paprika, bake in the oven for a further 10 minutes. Garnish with parsley.

This is the old wood-fired stove in my great grandfather's house, in Banja Luka. Hamid Dizdar built this house after they sold their country estate.

The meatballs always taste better from this stove.

Meatballs drenched in sauce.

SALATA OD MRKVE
CARROT SALAD

 10 minutes    30 minutes

5 Large Carrots
1 Cup Olive Oil
4 Cloves of Garlic
1 Bunch of Parsley
Juice of 1 Lemon
Salt (to taste)

Pepper (to taste)

Peel and cook the carrots, drain the water and set the carrots aside. Be careful not to overcook them, they should still keep a slight bite.

Place the cooked carrots in the olive oil. Finely chop the garlic, and mix through the olive oil and carrots.
Salt and pepper to taste.

It is always best to use lemons as the acidic component for these recipes. Too much vinegar, or too little, can ruin the flavour profile of a salad. Such a feat is much harder with the milder acidity of the lemon.

When The Chef was at culinary school, he suggested to his sister that she order a famous dish the next time she was out with her friends for lunch at a fine French restaurant.

Ever trusting, Edina ordered tomato concasse. The waiter looked flabbergasted, then affronted. Realising that she had been had, mum insisted that was in fact what she had always intended to order. When lunch was served all she had on her plate was a peeled and cooked tomato, forcing her to pretend she was on a diet.

Carrot salad drizzled with pumpkin oil.

MAHUNE
BROADBEANS

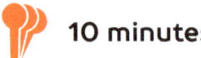 10 minutes    1 hour

1kg Broad Beans
5 Cloves of Garlic
1 Cup Cream
40g Butter
Salt (to taste)
Pepper (to taste)

You know that you have the right broad beans when you bend the pod and it snaps, rather than bends. Those beans are beautifully fresh and ready to be eaten. Cut the tops and bottoms from each bean and remove the string, if any. Then, slice the beans, if required, for the shape of your baking dish.

In a large pot of water, blanch the beans for a few minutes, then remove, and toss through with garlic, salt, pepper, and butter.

Place the mixture in your baking dish, cover with cream, and bake for 40 minutes.

Towards the end, gently dust the mixture either with flour and re-bake or simply cover with cream and re-bake for a further 20minutes. Or, my favourite: break up some ricotta cheese over the top and serve with a meaty dish.

The Chef's grandmother would make a broad bean stew, slow cooking with beef and spices, until both were soft. This sort of variant requires a hearty sprinkle with chopped garlic to best capture the autumnal flavours.

If you like a bit of spice in your life, blanch your beans with a chilli or two.

Just enough to pick up the spice without too much overpowering flavour.

Broiled and then baked, roast beans with garlic are a brilliant dish.

TUZLA PILE
SALT ROAST CHICKEN

 20 minutes  2 hours

1 large chicken
2kg salt
4 capsicums
10 egg whites
1 tbs peppercorns
1 cup water

Tuzla is a city in Bosnia that is famous for its salt mines. If you can get your hands on 2kg of their finest salt, I recommend you use it on this recipe.

Wash and then pat dry your chicken. Once dry, oil it thoroughly. Stuff the chicken with your favourite vegetables. I typically choose capsicums as they are quite fragrant and will infuse the chicken with their juices as it cooks.

Prepare the salt mixture by combining the salt and the egg whites. As required, add water to get a consistency of wet beach sand. Place the salt at the bottom of the baking dish, then your chicken, then, carefully, cover the chicken in the salt mixture ensuring that there are no pockets left open.

Bake the dish for 1 hour on 190° Celsius, and then for a further 1 hour on a very low heat. You may need a rolling pin to crack it open.

Nana used to cook pheasants in clay. She would not have approved of wasting salt.

When she was a child, during World War II, she would smuggle salt to share with different families.

Roast chicken, still encrusted in salt

PILE SA RIŽOM
ROAST CHICKEN PILAV

 10 minutes    1 hour

1 Chicken
2 Cups Rice
3 Cups Water
1 Carrot
1 Capsicum
2 Tbsp Vegeta

2 Tbsp Oil
1 Tbsp Pepper

Apply half the Vegeta to the chicken as a dry rub and roast the chicken in a deep dish for half an hour.

Chop the vegetables finely. In a large frying pan, heat up the oil, and quickly fry off the vegetables then add Vegeta and pepper. Add the 2 cups of rice, and then add 3 cups of water. Cover and allow to simmer gently for 20 minutes.

At the half hour mark, your chicken should be half done. Lift the chicken out of the dish, add the rice, and mix through with the chicken juices. Place the chicken onto the rice, cover with baking paper and foil, and then return back to the oven for a further half an hour.

The hotels in Banja Luka used to compete. Left over food was problematic both financially and morally as wasting food is always frowned upon. After one such banquet, piles of rice soaked in the beautiful roasting jus were left unserved. That evening, Nana's restaurant offered a one night only "Rice Pita".

Modern day leftovers typically make it into next day work lunches, but a spare half kilo of rice and some gravy will make a fine pita and a much more spectacular Monday lunch.

Roast chicken with pilav rice.

PATKA I OMAĆ
ROAST DUCK LINGUINE

 10 minutes    1 hour

1 Large Duck
300g Egg Linguine
2 Tbsp Vegeta
1 Bunch Parsley
1 Tbsp Salt

Rub the duck with the Vegeta and roast in the oven for 1 hour at 180° Celsius. Remove the duck and allow it to rest. Reserve the juices.

In a large pot, bring salty water to the boil and then add the linguine, being careful to give it a stir so that it does not stick. Cook the linguine till it is al dente and then toss through with the duck juices.

Serve the linguine in rounds, with the duck resting on top. Garnish with the parsley.

If Nana felt particularly loving, she would make this dish with one small change: instead of using store bought linguine, she would make a baked linguine from scratch and tear them into sheets called mlinci.

The recipe included 1 cup of flour, 1 tsp of salt, 1 egg, and a little bit of water per person. She would roll out the dough and then bake it on a stone tray for two minutes on each side. They would then be cooked much like a fresh pasta and rolled into the duck jus.

Roast duck served on a bed of linguine.

DOLMA

BREAD AND RICE CASSEROLE

 1 hour    2 hours

1 Old Boiler Chicken
1 Loaf Soda Bread
2 Cups Rice
4 Tbsp Pepper
2 Tbsp Vegeta

Cover the chicken in water and bring to the boil. Throw out the water, reserving the chicken, this will ensure you get a more clear broth.

Now use at least $2^{1/2}$ litres of water and bring the chicken to the boil a second time, add the Vegeta, and simmer for 2 hours, to create at least 2 litres of stock. Reserve the stock and the chicken. Make the recipe for soda bread (page 26) and crumble the bread on the bottom of a large casserole dish.

Cook 2 cups of rice in four cups of stock, using the absorption method. Aborio or Bomba rice are suitable for this dish. (The absorption method: place the rice and the stock in a pot, bring to the boil, stir once, and then put the lid on and allow the rice to simmer gently for half an hour until the water is fully absorbed). Place the warm rice on the soda bread already in the casserole dish.

Either shred or carve the chicken and place on top of the rice. Cover the mixture with the leftover stock and pepper heavily. If you want, you can incorporate the Sultan's Soup dish on the next page and only cook one chicken for both dishes.

Bread and Rice casserole with tomatoes and cracked pepper.

ŠILČIĆI SA BAMIJOM
MEAT SKEWERS WITH OKRA

 10 minutes    2 hours

400g Cubed Lamb
200g Okra
2 Red Capsicums
1 Onion
3 Tbsp Tomato Paste
2 Tbsp Paprika

1 Tbsp Vegeta
1 Lemon

Place the onion, lamb, and capsicum, on the skewers, alternating as you go. Add water to cover and bring to boil. In a bowl mix the tomato paste, Vegeta, sweet paprika and a little bit of water and add to the mixture. Cover the stew and cook for two hours.

Place the okra into boiling water with a slice of lemon and allow it to cook for five minutes. Rinse off with cold water making sure that no slimy residue stays on the okra.

Add the okra to the baking dish and leave uncovered to reduce for 20 minutes.

Serve with plenty of crunchy bread and lemon.

Most Bosnian okra dishes are made with dried okra as it was typically imported and very expensive. The Chef's family grew okra, but Nana was determined that it should still be dried before it was used.

Okra and meat skewers in red sauce.

BEGOVA ČORBA
THE SULTAN'S SOUP

 10 minutes    2 hours

1 Boiler chicken
3 Carrots
3 Egg Yolks
2 Potatoes
2 Cups Okra
1 Stick Celery

1 Cup Peas
1 Cup Cream
1 Bunch Parsley

Boil the chicken to create at least 2 litres of stock. Remove the chicken and strain the fats, which you can discard. Make sure to reserve the broth as it is the basis of your dish. Blanch the okra and then rinse to remove the residue. Set the okra aside. If you are using fresh large okra, chop it first as it should be the same size as the rest of the vegetables.

Remove the bones from the chicken, discard the skin, cube the chicken breast and return it to the broth. The rest of the meat can be used for the dolma dish on the previous page.

Allow the water to reduce and add vegetables finely cubed. Add parsley. Bring the soup to the table almost at boiling.

Prepare the Legir by whisking the cream and egg yolk well. Serve the egg yolk mixture at the table and spoon into each bowl. This will cook through the egg immediately.

I have been trying to get The Chef to teach me this recipe for well over a decade. While many variants of this dish exist, this one is my very favourite.

Kastel is the medieval fortress in Banja Luka, the hometown of the Chef and branches of our family.

Currently it is the home of a fantastic restaurant.

BAMIJA

OKRA

 10 minutes   3 hours

3 Lamb Shanks, Cut
2 Cups Okra
2 Onions
2 Carrots
1 Tbsp Vegeta
1 Lemon

Brown off the lamb shanks in a little bit of oil. Add the chopped onion, the chopped carrot, and the Vegeta. Cover with water and bring to the boil. Then, simmer for 3 hours, until the meat is soft and pulls away from the bone.

Blanch the okra and rinse off any residue with cold water. Place the okra in the stew and cook for a further 20 minutes.

Serve the two halves of the lamb shank per person, with a good helping of the stew and a slice or two of lemon.

Don't forget the maslenica or a crunchy bread.

If you are growing okra in the Bosnian style, you must pick them each morning so that they are the right size.

BOSANSKI LONAC
BOSNIAN STEW POT

 20 minutes  6 hours

500g Veal
500g Young Beef
Head of Cabbage
2 Carrots
1 Parsnip
1 Cup Peas

2 Tbsp Vegeta
2 Bay Leaves
1 Tbsp Hot Paprika

Chop and cube all the vegetables, except for the cabbage, which should be cut in wedges. Cube the meat and sprinkle with Vegeta.

In a large cast iron pot (or the slow cooker), layer first the cubed veal, then half the vegetables, then the young beef, then the rest of the vegetables. Sprinkle hot paprika. Add water to cover the stew and tie up with baking paper (or a heavy set lid). Bring the mixture to the boil and then simmer for 5-6 hours.

Serve with sour cream and beetroot slices.

There are many variants of this dish. The most heartbreaking variant, for me, was the ones mum made during the war. On some days, we cooked in old soup cans over open flame, in the defunct parking lots of the refugee camps in which we lived.

There must have been summer at some point in Travnik in 1994, but all I remember is snow, sleet, and rain.

The Chef had been conscripted and was working in the army kitchens, often gone for months at a time.

I wanted to ask him what he cooked and how he survived in that environment, but the look in his dark eyes always stopped me.

GULAŠ
GOULASH

 10 minutes   3 hours

500g Beef
2 Large Onions
2 Tbsp Tomato Paste
1 Tbsp Salt
1 Tbsp Pepper
1 Tbsp Oil

1 Tbsp Flour

Cube the beef, salt and pepper it, and then place it in the fridge. There should be just about the same volume of onion, finely chopped.

In a hot casserole dish, sweat the onions, and then when they are translucent add the meat, keep in mind that the meat will reduce the temperature in your pan and therefore add it slowly.

When the meat jus has receded, add the tomato paste and stir. That should start to fry as well. At that point, slowly add a spoonful of flour, which will thicken the goulash. Then, add water half a cup at a time, till the mixture has reached the right consistency.

To make Hungarian Goulash, add either chilli or hot paprika to the dish.

Goulash served with spinach and beetroot leaves.

GRAH
BEAN SOUP

 2 hours    2 hours

1kg Dried Beans
200g Smoked Beef Ribs
3 Cloves Garlic
2 Carrots
3 Tbsp Pepper
1 Onion

1 Bay Leaf

Soak the beans in water, preferably for a few hours. Drain the water and rinse the beans.

The dish works best with smoked beef bones, although it is perfectly reasonable to serve as a vegetarian dish, too. If you are using smoked beef, do not add any salt as the dish will be salty enough.

Chop and slice your vegetables.

Place the meat, vegetables, and the beans into either a slow cooker or a large cast iron pot, and cover with lukewarm water. Bring to the boil, and then reduce to a simmer for 2-4 hours.

You should be able to squash the beans between your fingers and the meat should pull off the bone. Serve the dish either with a drizzle of oil and a heavy dusting of cracked pepper, or, with a sunny side egg on top.

During the war all we ate was beans. I have only one happy memory of beans; sitting in a field in a village outside of Novi Travnik, with our Chef, shelling the dried beans out of their pods. Their colours and shapes vivid and bright and slipping through my fingers.

The only other way to eat bean soup is in reverse. Dig out the middle from your bread, and pour the soup inside.

Leftovers go into a bean stew bread and butter pudding.

KLEPE
DUMPLINGS

 30 minutes   30 minutes

1½ Cups Flour
1 Cup Mince
1 Egg
2 Tbsp Tomato Paste
1 Tbsp Sweet Paprika
1 Tbsp Vegeta

1 Tbsp Oil
1 Tsp Salt
1 Bunch Parsley
1 Cup Sour Cream

Mix the flour, egg, oil, salt, and water to create a dough. Roll the dough out to about 3mm in thickness and cut out either squares or rectangles, depending on how you like to fold your dumplings. Ours are folded the way you would an envelope, with a pinch in the middle.

Mix the mince and Vegeta to create the stuffing mixture. Carefully spoon 1 tbs of the mixture per dumpling and bring in the edges to meet in the middle.

In a large pot, bring to the boil 4 cups of water, 2 tbsp of tomato paste, 1 tbsp of sweet paprika. Place the dumplings one by one into to the soup. Once all the dumplings are in the soup, cook for a further five minutes at a rolling boil and then remove.

It is possible to thicken this soup with the sauce mentioned in previous pages, by adding 2 tbsp of flour to half a cup of oil and browning off the sauce in a separate pan.

To that you can add 1 cup of water and then cook until thickened. Whilst it certainly makes the dish very decadent, it is in this instance best left for winter stews.

Klepe was the start of my love for ravioli. Here two worlds could meet.

Bosnians typically don't make klepe from spinach and cheese, but I have found it to be as wonderful as any ravioli.

Try that variant too.

Klepe served with sour cream.

MEDENO MESO
HONEYED MEAT

 30 minutes  2 hours

500g Beef
500g Prunes
1 Knob Butter
1 Tbsp Vegeta

Soak 500g of prunes in a large pot of water. Throw away the water but reserve the prunes.

Cube the beef and dry rub with Vegeta.

In a large cast iron post, fry the beef in the butter till it is browned off. Add the prunes to the dish, cover with cold water and bring to the boil.

Cook at a simmer for 2 hours, until the meat is soft.

This was the dish created by my Nana for a culinary event in Banja Luka. Such dishes were the cause of her winning three gold medals at the different culinary events, including the Mediterranean culinary Olympics. Interestingly, the dish contains no honey, the sweetness is entirely derived from the prunes.

Competing against this dish was the Chef with his offering from page 42.

Our Chef had come in Bronze; losing out to Nana (who got gold, as always) and to his teacher (who attained silver and was the head Chef at Hotel Palas in Banja Luka).

RIPA
SWEDES

 30 minutes   2 hours

1kg Casserole Beef
200g Smoked Ribs
1kg Swede
1 Tbsp Vegeta
1 Tbsp Sweet Paprika
Pepper (to taste)

Blanch the smoked ribs and discard the water.

Cube the beef and brown off in a large cast iron pot. Add the smoked ribs, and cover with water. Bring the dish to boil and then reduce to a simmer for two hours.

Once the meat is soft, slice the swede and add to the pot. Sprinkle with Vegeta and sweet paprika and cook until the swede gives way when you pinch it.

For the connoisseur inclined toward molecular gastronomy, swede foams and soups work wonderfully with slow cooked ox cheek.

An iSi Whipper is an essential tool if you are looking at modernising this dish. Slow cook the meats and the swede, as above, but keep the proteins and the vegetables separate. Then, create the swede foam with your iSi Whipper and serve on a bed of crunchy sprouts.

Swede and smoked beef.

TRAHANA
SOURDOUGH SOUP

 20 minutes    30 minutes

200g Beef Mince
3 Tbsp Tomato Paste
1 Tbsp Vegeta
4 Cups Water
Pepper (to taste)
Parsley

1 Tbsp Cream

Trahana is a sourdough soup pasta popular throughout Greece, Turkey, and the Balkans.

To make it from scratch you will need 2 cups of flour, 1 tbs of salt, fresh yeast, a tomato, making sure that you remove the seeds and skin and 1 cup of warm water.

Mix that thoroughly into a dough and leave overnight at room temperature. This should make the dough start to sour and rise.

The next day add flour to the dough so that the mixture is hard and firm. Rub through either a colander or a custom made pan, so that small pieces of the dough fall away. This is often made in summer and dried on large dedicated table cloths.

Trahana is also easily bought in most delicatessens. To make the soup, fry the mince in a large pot. Add to that the tomato paste, the Vegeta, and the water.

Once the water is boiling, add $1/3$ of a cup of dry trahana, and cover. Cook the soup for a further fifteen minutes.

Serve with cream and parsley.

Making trahana was a huge and inescapable childhood chore, that I dearly miss now.

It is a great way to be mindful and present, and really connect with your food.

ĆEVAPI

SKINLESS SAUSAGE

 24 hours   8 minutes

600g Young Beef Chuck
400g Lamb
5 Cloves Garlic
½ Cup Oil
1 Tbsp Salt

There are as many recipes for this dish as there are towns and villages in Europe. Our Chef prefers to make it as follows: Use two types of meat preferably 600g of young beef and 400g of lamb. Choose a fattier meat (10% fat minimum, 20% would be better).

Cube the meat and salt it. Place it in a marinating dish, and add the garlic and oil. Rest in the fridge for 24 hours.

Mince the meat and the garlic. If you do not own a mincer, you can buy minced meat and rest it salted with minced garlic and oil for the same period.

Work the mixture until the proteins are elastic and the fat coats your hands. Wash your hands, oil them, then form into sausages. At that point you can either fry, grill, BBQ, keeping in mind that coals are always best.

Serve in lepina with sour cream and onions. Add freshly cracked pepper at the end.

The version from Sanski Most includes 3 tbs of freshly cracked pepper in the mixture and is formed into the shape of a dukat (old coin currency).

It is a small rissole, fried, and the lepina is entirely soaked in the meat jus. In Banja Luka the skinless sausages are pressed into the shape of a patty so that you cook four at a time.

PLJESKAVICA
BURGER PATTIE

 24 hours    15 minutes

600g Young Beef Chuck
400g Lamb
5 Cloves Garlic
½ Cup Oil
1 Tbsp Salt
1 Onion

Cracked Pepper

Made similarly as the skinless sausage from the previous page, this dish also includes a finely chopped onion added at the time of mixing. It is formed into large and thin hamburger patties, usually the size of a small bread plate. It makes the most fantastic burger with shredded cabbage and a spicy ketchup, or served traditionally with ajvar, sour cream, and hot pickled fafarone.

The version from Leskovac, Serbia, includes the fafarone in the patty and is quite spicy. For that variant, we recommend you serve it with a lot of sour cream.

For a quick pickle, place hot chillies in a small jar and add 1 tbs of salt, 1 tbs of sugar, and 1 cup of vinegar. Keep in the fridge for 6 hours to 1 week. They are commonly canned for winter and eaten with a variety of dishes.

If you're no good with the thin patty, Tahira Dizdar, our Chef's grandmother cooked her patties with a shallow hole in the middle. This ensured that the juices that bubble to the top fold back in.

It is technically a different dish, but never mind that. Add cheese instead.

Pljeskavica with sour cream, onions, and ajvar.

ŠIŠ ĆEVAP
SKEWERED ĆEVAP

 24 hours    10 minutes

600g Young Beef Chuck
400g Lamb
5 Cloves Garlic
½ Cup Oil
1 Tbsp Salt
Pepper (to taste)

This variant of the dish is usually much larger and gets its name from the skewer in the middle. Traditionally it would be served in a lepina, as pictured, and eaten in dedicated restaurants throughout Bosnia.

We quite enjoy serving it at events as it is very party friendly. It forms a great basis for street food and night markets and is easier to maneuver over the coals.

The party variant looks a little different. The meat is made slightly shorter, and once mostly cooked, bread slices are added to the ends and the skewer is then returned to the coals, allowing the bread to toast and the meat to finish cooking.

Making these dishes is a calling, and whilst each family often makes their own, we also buy them to cook at home from our favourite butchers and then go out to lunch and order them from specialty restaurants.

Always serve in a lepina.

PAŠTETA
PÂTÉ

 10 minutes

1 Cup shredded Chicken
½ Cup Butter
1 Tbsp Pepper
1 Tbsp Salt

Pâté is the most common breakfast dish of my childhood. It is available to purchase in every store, in a can, and is made by dozens of companies with dozens of recipes.

Many mothers from the Balkans also made their own, and would pack it for their children as a respectable lunch down at the riverbank, or whatever mischief we were getting into. Typically you spread it on bread and eat it with either a tomato, onion, capsicum, or some combination of each.

We make pâté when ever there is leftover chicken. Roasted, boiled, from the BBQ, whatever you have.

Shred 1 cup of the chicken and for best results, either add the gelatin you got from the stock or add ½ cup of butter. I typically use some cholesterol reducing spread. Then, blend the mixture in a food processor and add salt and pepper to taste.

Grab some bread, a tomato, pack your bags, and head down to the beach.

Always best served with Turkish bread and cracked pepper.

SIR
RICOTTA CHEESE

 20 minutes  1 hour

4 Litres Milk
3 Tbsp Vinegar
1 Tbsp Salt

Making ricotta cheese is incredibly simple and this recipe is a wonderful start for any of the dishes in this book that include ricotta.

Place a colander into a large bowl and a cheese cloth over that. Pour boiling water over the cloth and the colander, and carefully drain out of the pot.

In a large pot bring 4L of milk to 76° Celsius. Add the vinegar and wait for the milk to start to curdle. Once it has fully separated, drain the curds and the whey into the cheese cloth.

The colander should stop the cloth form running away. The pot should save the whey for either bread making or any number of other sensible uses.

Bring together the ends of the cheese cloth. I usually use a wooden spoon to twist the cloth into a ball to drain the curds. Salt to taste.

Please reserve as much of the whey as you can. It can be used in a variety of baking, instead of water as you are making bread, or as a started for a second cheese.

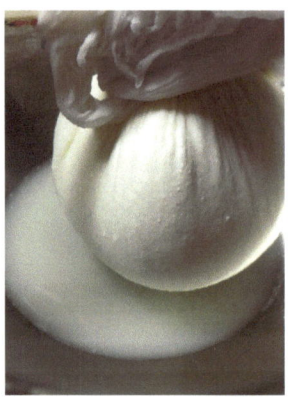

Ricotta cheese in cheesecloth with a bottle of whey.

SIRILUK
SPRING ONION DIP

 15 minutes

500g Ricotta Cheese
1 Bunch Spring Onion
½ Cup Cream
Chives to Garnish
Salt (to taste)

Wash and chop the spring onion.

In a large bowl add the spring onion to the cheese and salt to taste. Depending on what soft cheese you are using and how liquid it is, you may need to add some cream or sour cream to help the mixture stay together. For added decadence grate 200g of feta cheese into the mixture.

Form the mixture into balls and roll the balls in a dish of finely chopped chives to garnish.

Serve either as a dip or with meaty dishes.

If you are making this dish consider also making the ricotta from scratch from the previous page.

Siriluk is a family favourite and I could not imagine a barbecue without it.

Onion and ricotta dip with chives.

BUDIMKA

ROAST PUMPKIN

 10 minutes    15 minutes

1 Roasting Pumpkin
1 Cup Runny Apple Jam

Wash, cut in half, and place the pumpkin in a roasting tray. Roast at 200° Celsius for 25 minutes, or until the pumpkin is cooked through and caramelised on top.

The sweetness of the pumpkin is brought out with runny apple jam (or plum jam) and is delicious. A dusting with powdered sugar and cinnamon would take this very simple dish to a proper homage to autumnal flavours.

It is common to serve roasted pumpkin and jam to late night guests.

Lunch is typically the main meal in Bosnia and suppers range from as simple and light as this one, to more complicated affairs, but always as a second fiddle to the more important family meal.

I suspect you could get a free meal in any Bosnian home by asking if there is "bujrum" (it means welcome).

Immediately you are ushered inside, given slippers, and fed.

Roast pumpkin with apple jam.

GRIZ
SEMOLINA PUDDING

 5 minutes 15 minutes

500ml Milk
4 Tbsp Sugar
3 Tbsp Semolina
1 Vanilla Pod
Cinnamon Sugar

Bring the milk to the boil and reduce the heat to simmering. Add the vanilla to the milk, then the sugar, and then the semolina. Stir and keep the mixture moving until the semolina thickens.

Cook for 15 minutes until a creamy texture is achieved. If it burns at the bottom, the flavour will mix through the dish and be inedible.

While it is runny, you can pour the semolina into a variety of dishes. Once it cools, it will thicken further, and often form a film on top.

To serve you can dust with cinnamon alone, cinnamon sugar, vanilla sugar, or chocolate, for an added kick. Layers of fruit or whipped cream are also a lovely touch.

The pudding can be served warm or cool and was a favourite of mine whenever I was home sick from school.

Three of my favourite pudding varieties, chocolate, cinnamon, and vanilla sugar.

HALVA
SHORTBREAD ROUNDS

 10 minutes   20 minutes

2 Cups Flour
2 Cups Sugar
2 Cups Water
1 Cup Melted Butter
½ Cup Oil

Melt the oil and butter in a large pan. Then, fry the flour in the oil and butter mixture until golden brown. Boil the water and sugar. Add the boiling mixture into the flour, cook until the mixture comes away from the pan. Serve as little balls.

When the Chef was just a little lad, four or five, he had woken in the night, and asked Nana for something to eat. "Is there a little bit of halva?" He had murmured.

Like any Bosnian mother for her favourite youngest son, Nana promptly got her pots and pans out, and over the still-warm wood fire stove, made some halva.

When he was full and content, the Chef sleepy rolled over and said "leave the rest for Sister." and went to sleep. This was such a popular anecdote in our family, that two generations later and we still quote it when someone is asking for something sweet to indulge in.

The Chef tells me that he first asked, "Is there any meat?", but it is too late for him to salvage this story now.

Halva, served with walnuts and plums.

JABUKE U ŠLAFRUKU
APPLE FRITTERS

 20 minutes    10 minutes

3 Large Apples
1 Elderflower Blossom
1 Cup Oil
1 Cup Icing Sugar

2 Tbsp Flour
1 Egg
Pinch of Salt

Peel and core the apples and slice into 1½ cm thick round slices. Heat the oil in a deep frying pan.

Each slice of apple, should be battered, first in the egg, then in the flour and salt mixture, and then fried till golden.

Drain the excess oil by placing the apple slices on bunches of paper towels and then serve dusted with icing sugar and elderflower blossoms. If you have no elderflower blossom, use hibiscus or apple tea. Dried lavender with the icing sugar is also an amazing option.

For elderflower cordial, you will need 21 elderflower blooms. Wash each blossom cluster and put them in a large pot and sprinkle heavily with sugar. Leave overnight. Boil the mixture and add more sugar until the mixture is thick. Once boiled you have the cordial. The Chef and I made elderflower cordial every summer I was in Bosnia; spending the sun drenched mornings picking the blooms on the river bank, laughing and startling the dragonflies.

Apple fritters with icing sugar.

KADAIF

KADAIF CAKE

 20 minutes   1 hour

500g Kadaif
500g Ground Walnuts
250g Butter
5 Cups Sugar

4 Cups Water
1 Vanilla Sugar
1 Lemon

Vanilla sugar is a popular addition to a lot of modern Bosnian dishes. It is sold in little sachets, although it can be made quite easily by placing vanilla pods into a container with caster or plain sugar.

Kadaif is a noodle like dish, and in many countries can be added to savoury food to create interesting textures, much like any other pastry.

In Bosnia, it is typically only used as a dessert.
Place half the kadaif mixture in a well greased baking dish.

Mix the walnuts, 1 cup sugar, and vanilla, lemon rind in a separate dish. Then, distribute the walnut mixture on top of the kadaif in the baking dish, and gently pres down with your hand.

On top of the walnut layer, place the rest of the kadaif.

Cover the layers with the melted butter and bake at 160° Celsius until golden brown.

Make the simple syrup by mixing the 4 cups sugar, water, and 2 slices of lemon. Bring that to the boil. Pour the sugar syrup over the kadaif and allow to rest for an hour for the liquid to be absorbed.

Cut the kadaif into cubes.

Try wrapping the kadaif around any number of things, like stewed apples, or something savoury such as chicken. I have had it with prawns and lamb, and it was fantastic.

Kadaif before it is cut.

The Lost Chef - Page 132

KAHVA I SEĆER
COFFEE AND SUGAR

 10 minutes    1 minute

20g Ground Coffee
1 Cup Water
Sugar Cubes
Milk

Place the coffee grounds in the džezva (little copper coffee pot) and hold that over the heat, allowing it to roast a little bit in the dry coffee pot.

Add boiling water to the coffee, stir, and then place on the hot stove or 60 seconds or until the mixture has hiccuped.

Immediately remove from the heat or it will boil over creating a fantastic mess.

Serve in little coffee cups (fildžan) with milk.

Traditionally, complicated pouring rituals existed. Daughters in law would make coffee for the whole family, grinding the beans early that morning. It is common for many families to roast their own coffee still.

Sugar cubes are served and you are expected to sip your coffee through the cube.

Milk is often boiled for hours until cream collects on top, and that is then spooned into your cup with the coffee.

ŠAPE
SHORTBREAD

 15 minutes   25 minutes

1½ Cups Flour
1½ Cups Dessicated Coconut
1 Cup Butter
1 Cup Icing Sugar

½ Cup Caster Sugar
1 Egg
1 Tbsp Sour Cream

Add all the ingredients except for the icing sugar and mix well. It should create a crumb similar to that of shortbread. Press the mixture into cookie moulds. In a pinch, a muffin pan will do fine.

Bake on a low heat for an hour, until golden. Immediately remove from the trays and cool on cooling racks.

Dust with icing sugar and serve with peppermint tea.

In Bosnia, peppermint tea is a household staple although it is usually served with sugar (or honey) and can be wonderfully sweet.

Most herbal teas and tisanes are well regarded and drank with an almost medical precision. Working on this book, the Chef and I had spent an eternity talking through the recipes, with cups of rose-hip or chamomile tea.

During the war, Nana would take me into the woods to teach me how to harvest various roots, herbs, and tree bark scrapings to make medicinal teas.

Shortbread with icing sugar.

SUTLIJE
RICE PUDDING

 10 minutes   30 minutes

500ml Milk
½ Cup Risotto Rice
4 Tbsp Sugar

Bring the milk to the boil and add in the sugar and risotto rice. Stir continuously for 20 minutes, until the mixture has thickened and the rice softened. Cover with the lid and reduce the temperature for a further 10 minutes. The rice should be soft and the pudding runny. Sultanas, figs, or any very sweet fruit will work beautifully with this rice pudding.

Nana often made sutlije as it was a family favourite (except our Chef). I include it here so that I can share with you this story: When the Chef was young, his paternal grandparents lived in Kotor Varoš, where he would go visit from time to time. The Dizdars owned the shopping mall in town and also kept some farm animals on their estate, including a cow or two. Our Chef, as a toddler, once remarked in absolute amazement to his grandmother "at home milk comes in a bottle, but your milk comes from cows".

We saw there the early abandonment of the paddock to table lifestyle. It startles me because most people I now know buy rice pudding in little jars.

TUFAHIJE
STUFFED APPLES

 20 minutes   1 hour

4 Cooking Apples
2L Water
1kg Sugar
1 Cup Whipped Cream
100g Ground Walnuts
½ Cup Milk

Cherries in Syrup
Vanilla Sugar
1 Slice of Lemon
Chocolate shavings

Peel and core the apples, but make sure to keep them whole and unblemished. Add the water in a large pot, with sugar, vanilla and a slice of lemon. When the mixture boils, place the apples in and cook the apples until soft. Remove the apples from the water and allow them to cool.

Cook the ground walnuts in the milk until the mixture thickens a little. Set aise and once it has cooled enough to handle, fill the apple centre with the mixture.

Cover the top with whipped cream and serve with a cherry and a dusting of chocolate shavings.

It would have been a shame to deconstruct this dish simply to modernise it. We flirted with the idea of it for a few tries, but the silhouette of the apple and cream felt almost representative of the nostalgia that is felt by the displaced Bosnian people and so we staid true to tradition.

If you are feeling particularly adventurous, and have an ice cream churning machine on hand, this dish would make a spectacular ice cream to be served on ground walnuts with chocolate syrup.

Apples stuffed with walnuts and covered in cream.

HURMAŠICE
SHORTBREAD IN SYRUP

 10 minutes    30 minutes

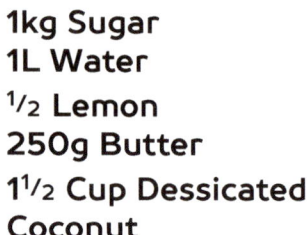

1kg Sugar
1L Water
½ Lemon
250g Butter
1½ Cup Dessicated Coconut

1½ Cup Flour
½ Cup Caster Sugar
⅓ Cup Oil
1 Egg, 1 Egg Yolk
1 Tbsp Sour Cream

Melt the butter and then mix in the oil and sugar. Whip until it is foamy and light. Add the eggs, sour cream, and fold gently.

Add the flour and coconut and mix until it forms a ball that pulls away from the dish.

Make into finger sized shapes and press into a grater to create the pattern.

Bake on a gentle heat for 30 minutes until golden and allow to cool.

Make the simple syrup by mixing the sugar, water, lemon and brining to the boil. Cover the golden shortbread with the hot syrup and allow it to soak.

In our family, when a baby would begin to walk, the mother would bake a tray of these shortbreads and invite the family over for lunch to celebrate.

The little one would walk across the tray, and the person they walked towards would get the whole tray (most of which would then be eaten at the luncheon).

Shortbread in syrup. Ready for a walking baby.

PALAČINKE
CRÊPES

 10 minutes    1 minute

2 Cups Flour
2 Cups Milk
2 Eggs
1 Tbsp Baking Powder
⅓ Cup Oil
Pinch of Salt

Pinch of Sugar
Toppings
Aerosol Oil

Mix the ingredients until you get a runny batter. You can keep the batter in the fridge, to allow the glutens to rest, or, if you are in a rush, just skip the resting step.

Heat a shallow non stick frying pan with a little bit of butter.

Pour gently ⅓ of a cup of the batter and allow for the mixture to coat the pan.

The moment little bubbles have formed and burst the underside is cooked and is ready to flip. If you have not done this before, use a spatula to flip the crepe.

Expect the first crepe to fail. The second will work out fajn (The Bosnian word for 'fine', with the emphasis on good).

Typically serve with walnuts, hazelnuts, and melted chocolate. Or cheese and onion.

As children, we would travel to Croatia for the best pancakes to be had. Everyone in Bosanska Gradiška just called the other side of the Sava "Across" and it was considered perfectly sensible to make the drive for pancakes. The drive would now require four border crossings and a passport.

It is terrible to say, but my favourite pancakes were in Tokyo. I await for Bosnia to start serving them as street food and encourage each and every person to set up a pancake cart straight away.

Crêpés, served with walnuts, strawberry jam, tomato jam, ajvar, and chocolate.

About the Author

Leila Chalk nee Lejla Bošnjak is a lawyer and a cook. She is the child of two worlds, having been born in Australia, she grew up in Bosnia from 1986 till mid 1994. Her family, including our Chef, moved as refugees, mostly in camps, for the entirety of the war; Bosanksa Gradiška, Banja Luka, Zagreb, Novi Travnik, Travnik, Bugojno. In 1994, Leila and her immediate family escaped the war and lived in a detention camp in Varaždin, Croatia, for fifteen months. A further two years of international post refugee re-settlement dramas in Australia and Bosnia, before they finally settled in Melbourne, Australia, in late 1997. There, Leila studied, loved, laughed, cooked, and finally, wrote.

Hajro Dizdar

Andrew Chalk